Megha Jain is a student, writer, and traveller. She has written this book from personal experiences and observed relationships and has come to realise that humans of today are struggling way too much than our fragile hearts were not ready for. This work is for anyone struggling with mental health issues, insecurities and transitioning into adulthood. Anyone who is learning to adult; starting work, moving in or out of relationships, friendships, places, and most of all getting to know themselves. She has gone through all these things to be able to share this book with you and hopes that this becomes your room away from the world when you just need space and comfort. Best advice: grab a glass of your favourite drink and read away.

I would like to dedicate this book to you, the growing and living of you

Megha Jain

ADULTING

AUSTIN MACAULEY PUBLISHERS™

LONDON • CAMBRIDGE • NEW YORK • SHARJAH

A CIP catalogue record for this title is available from the British Library.

ISBN 9781035801961 (Paperback)
ISBN 9781035801978 (ePub e-book)

www.austinmacauley.com

First Published 2023
Austin Macauley Publishers Ltd®
1 Canada Square
Canary Wharf
London
E14 5AA

I would like to thank my family, sisters and friends, my therapist and Austin Macauley for giving me an opportunity to become an author.

relationships past and the future

i have realised that
the idea of love
is a little flawed
you see,
falling in love
with someone is not it
you fall in love with your friends
and things
and places
it's the kind of love that
remains constant in your life
it heals
it supports,
and most of all it understands
i know secretly you are waiting
for the right person at the right time
but don't crave for love too much
it comes when it has to
it'll be quick and slow at the same time
it might end soon
or last till your forever
but for now
fall in love with things
and people
and the sky
and your favourite colour
fall in love with every version of you.

i was looped
into the idea of love
two people, dating who may not
entirely deserve each other but are still together
i was dating throughout
high school
balancing between friends
school
and a boyfriend
i thought this was it
that life is just a balancing act
in order for it to work for you
but now when i am adulting
i am growing
without being held back by a relationship
i am exploring
indulging
and reflecting
i am getting to know myself again
but i sometimes wonder
if the old parts of me will ever recover from
loving and being loved
by another.

i was
free falling in love
until i realised
it was a dream
i often thought about
love,
being in love
being so right for someone
that the wrongs
never seem to exist
being honest in love
to yourself and them
like you live in a
glass house
but never blind in love
you see
i learnt that sometimes
the distance grows
the misery of moving on
and the healing of a
broken heart
takes more of you
than you were ready for
you see
love of any kind can
break you;
friendships and relationships
but only you can damage you
and as much as you try to repair it
a small part of that damage persists
until you learn to love yourself.

it's funny how we haven't talked in months
but i still know what makes you smile
i remember how the lines on your forehead changed
as your moods changed, like it was yesterday
i remember what it feels like to hold your hand,
not entirely soft but just enough to keep mine warm
i remember how you swear when you're angry
and how you never know when to shut up
all these little things
waiting to be replaced by someone else's little things because
i also remember
how lying to me was so simple for you
how my misery didn't affect you as much
because you were in your head too
how you always needed me
but never made me feel like i need you
i remember you claiming to love me and i not
when we ended things.

i want you to be more than just a text every day
i want to listen to stories that are your sweetest memories
i want you to reminisce your schooldays with me
i want to know about your new friends
and how your day was
tell me about your first kiss
your first failure and your success
let me in on some of your secrets
and i'll tell you a few
tell me the story about that scar on your forehead
tell me about your regrets
your dreams
and your beliefs
let's dance in our bedroom
and sing on the kitchen table
let's sit under the stars while the world moves on
and i'll hold onto those memories when you are away
when i miss you
i'll have those memories to sleep away on a lonely night
i know you are just a facetime away
but i can't fight with you on a screen
i want to be angry and then
fall into your arms to cry
because we said things we didn't mean
i want to touch you
and feel your warmth
so tell me baby, will you travel the distance?
or maybe meet me halfway
to make some promises
of forever.

do you miss me
when you are in a room full of people
but i am not in the crowd?
do you miss me
on days when you are happy
and in your sad moments?
do you miss me
while doing small things in the day
like brushing your teeth
or driving your car
or doing the dishes?
because i do
i miss you
and my heart hopes a little
but more than that
my mind fools me
into believing
the missing will stop
when i find you.

i have a little more to say
than you are willing to listen
i want to travel and fall in love
but not like the movies
i want to live like a youngster
till i get old
i want to share and grieve with you
because i know you'll need me
a little more as we grow
and me too, sometimes
i don't want you to be
frail as we age
i want us to be oldies who kiss
while passing by
and give hugs like its routine
and take turns to carry grocery bags on our way home because
yes, i over bought
but by now you've gotten used to it
so you always carry an extra bag
i want to share holidays, kids
and treasures of my life with you
and i hope you remember
the life we had as we grow old
and let it only fade
into photographs for others
when we meet at our grave.

waiting for you is like waiting for a shooting star on a cloudy
night
sleepless
i wait from dusk till dawn everyday
hoping
for you to be mine someday
reaching
to the skies and all element
desperately
waiting for you

i am tired
and my bones are shaking
and my mind keeps telling me things
i don't want to hear
so i listen to the rain
outside my window
in hope that they tell me stories about us
about a someday when atoms of us are together
when the tides rise higher to reach the undisturbed sand, when
the sky turns into canvas
that the sun and the moon paint together
i am running from my mind and towards my heart
at every beat the strides are stronger
i run naked from shore to shore
madness, people say
love, i think

my body suddenly aware of my escaping soul in search of its
mate
the wind pushing me against my destination

because the trees know the truth
so i swim across not oceans but feelings
madness, people say
love, i think
i find myself running with all the strength that i could gather
that my heart forgets why and my mind floods with memories
of us
only to realise that my purpose is lost
that you were gone

believing
that the universe broke into galaxies to keep us apart
and the sun and the moon can never reach but only long
the sea and the sky can never meet but only indulge in long
conversations
and i have to now pick up the pieces of my broken body to
feed my soul
madness, people say
love, i think
as my lungs gasp for air
i find myself knelt down on the wet mud
the trees around me growing taller
and the earth pulling me down

and i hear you
only my imagination could fool me that way
listening to your voice as i long for it

i see you've come to say goodbye
to my empty heart
i rest my eyes and i feel the rain on my skin

the sky is crying with me today
as i bid farewell to you

so now i come here
sometimes when i miss you
to listen to your voice again
and feel your warmth from the ground
as i lay next to your grave
love, people say
madness, i think.

my parents raised me
to be a hopeless romantic
so i was always looking for the one
in corners and alleys i crossed
but there is no such thing as 'the one'

people hold many designations
a lover
a friend
an acquaintance
a therapist
a parent
a mentor
a sibling
so searching for 'the one'
is not for this generation

i refuse to believe that
only one person
deserves all my love
and are ready to give all of theirs
and between that,
the adjustments we make
and settle into comfortable patterns
with a love that might not be love

i fear giving myself to someone
like my mom did to my dad
and my dad did to my mom
i fear i'll lose myself
in the process of giving

the idea of love is interesting
but what if
i've already moved on from the one?
what if i can't have them?
what if i am the one for myself
and all along i was looking for someone else?

so i keep half of my heart for myself
and the other half,
i break into pieces
for people in my life
who hold those designations
and deserve a very unfiltered part of my love.

home is
white butterflies on pink dahlias
my pup playing with a deflated ball
that remains in the garden at all times

home is
where i grow sunflowers
or at least try to
my pup grows into a lazy dog
and he moves on from that ball

home is
movie marathons on a weekday
even though we shouldn't
and friday dinner dates
and spring garden picnics

home is
our babies tearing
paper wrapping apart on christmas
and learning to bike
on the house street

home is
dishes breaking
and dreadful laundry days
and kids falling and crying
and teenager's wilding

home is
where we make love

and share love
and grow together
but not apart

home is
wherever you are with
me under a roof
counting stars
not days.

i am taking my love
and keeping it in your palms
you decide
if you want to hold onto it
or let it go.

i hug myself at night
in order to sleep
and on more difficult days
i tell myself
that everything is going to be okay
while grazing my fingers on my back
i soon realised,
i had to be enough for myself
because i had no one
neither was i looking
because the one i wanted
i didn't know yet
so i decided to eat with a candle lit
like i was on a date everyday
i decided to wrap myself
in a cosy blanket
on my sofa when i needed a cuddle.
i was enough
and it took me a long time
to understand
that loving myself was enough.

my nerves became background noise
and i made no attempt to give in
as unfiltered conversations with your eyes
was something i wanted more intently
while our hands flirted,
our pace slowed
and our walls disintegrated
little by little,
we laid bricks again
only this time
we built a home,
not walls.

it's funny
how my heart
and my mind
are thinking about you
and for the first time
they agree with each other.

i'm losing the ability
to receive love
your arms
they hold me tight
but all i feel is
empty
maybe
tomorrow i will learn
to feel love again.

anxiety and depression

i boarded a sinking ship
thinking i'll survive
but turns out
i didn't have the strength
to swim to the shore
or call for help
it was too late by then
and i was drowning
the water filling my lungs
and my body turning cold
i finally settle deep under
lifeless, in an ocean full of life.

yes, it is one of those days
when i feel like
my body is making me uncomfortable
when i feel lonely
when i question my existence
when i let my mind take turns
and dig into my past or even my present
when i need someone
to just tell me
it is going to be okay
and pick me up
from where i left off all the rights in my life
just to stress about the wrongs.

i probably feel things 10 times more
than people normally do
that is why i also give more of myself
to you
but at this point
i am tired of giving
fighting
and expecting that for only a day
you will give some of you to me
i am aware
i live off people's validation
because i am unable to feel what words of wisdom i tell
myself
but do i really need to ask for affection?
ask to receive only a few drops for survival
when i can share the whole ocean
with someone else
do i really need to ask you to be here
when you know i need you?

did i tell you about the time
when i lived in my mind,
it was fucking awful.

i scream for help
but i am underwater,
i cry
and cry
and cry some more
because i have this feeling of melancholy
or am i just lonely?
i feel like everyone is saying the right words
like "i am here"
but it is like i am stuck
knee deep in quicksand, feeling numb
slowly
and watching everything around me move
forward or backwards
but move
and i can't find a way to come out of it
but it is just the earth pulling me back from where i came
and then i tell my mind to stop overthinking
stop harassing my body for a response
and i say to myself,
think happy thoughts.
before my palpitations
start making me dizzy
before i let myself believe
it is all not worth it
before i fall again
harder
and with injuries
i cannot recover from.

i am hurting because
i loved selflessly
i am hurting
not because i wasn't loved back
or i couldn't feel it
but because i lost myself
in the process of loving and caring
and, now, whenever i sit alone
i only wonder
how empty i feel
and the numbness
never goes away,
it remains
in varying intensities
but i can never completely feel
the wholeness that once lived in my heart
that has left home for another.

sunrises sometimes feel like betrayal
and sunsets are often feared
there have been nights longer than days
and days i did not wish to wake
i feel like a glass completely empty
and if the tremors are strong enough
breakable easily
sometimes it feels like the air isn't enough
to stop my suffocation
and smaller breaths repeat faster
it's not like sweaty palms and racing hearts
it's more like deafening ears and tired lungs
my mind pacing so fast
that i can't catch a thought but only feel numb
inside out from all this chaos
and while i stand
in front of my reflection
the cold mirror
against my forehead

makes it go away
for just a second
and a wave comes crashing
from the back of my mind
just to trickle down my cheeks
again and again
on different cold surfaces
but the same crashing thud.

why is it that even when
i am in all the right places
i don't feel happy?
just this constant nothingness
in my body
and at the back of my mind
always fighting the urge to fall apart
is it that hard?
to be happy?
to feel?
i feel like there is always
a grey cloud
right above me
even on the sunny days
and sometimes it drifts away
but i think the winds
are not my friend
because they push it right above my head
waiting for me to rain on floors, corners
and sometimes shoulders
funny, i feel all these feelings
but they are always racing each other
that i actually miss to recognise them
and always feel empty
because none of the good ones
make it to the finish line.

i am a tiny rock
that the waves keep crashing into
wave by wave abrading me
until i am only sediment
stripping me of my feelings
and only leaving me with
melancholy
i was unaware
of this constant hurting
and now
i am just a heartbeat away
from a breakdown.

i am not lonely
i am just tired of the world
making me feel like it
so, yeah, sometimes
i cry a lot
and feel like
i am underwater
losing my breath slowly
but then someone
throws me a life jacket
and i am still drowning
in the same ocean
only this time
i swim back up to gasp for air
only this time
it feels like i can survive
and someone jumped
to bring me back to the surface
only this time
i am not alone.

i was not in love with you
so i didn't really fall out of love
i was with you
because
you made me happy and i needed that
i thought along the way
i will learn to love
to be in love with you
but by the end
i was exhausted
giving so much of me
to be happy
that it made me sad
i was your punching bag
and your pillow
but i was just never enough
and so i left
just like that,
for myself.

there was a time
when i cried everyday
in my bed
or the shower
in my car
or the kitchen floor
every damn where
i left traces of tears
and just craved their presence
and i hate that it ended
abruptly
i hate that i couldn't love myself,
but only other people
i hate that i told myself
that i was overthinking it
when my feelings told me
otherwise
i hate that i didn't ask for love
and didn't limit myself
to love
i hate that whenever you come up in conversations
i still feel something
i hate that you have that power over me
and when i see you
all over again, the same story
i don't want to feel this anymore
the suffocation
the unworthiness
and always looking for validation
i don't want to feel this heart hurting
i want it to stop

all of it
the melancholy
the anxiety
the racing minds
and a pleading heart.

i was so sad
for all this time
that when i truly laughed sitting across her
with her
i felt happy
after a very long
time it felt so real
that i let a tear out
because that feeling was so unknown
even liberating for that moment
i wish i could say
i am happy
but no feeling is constant
we work on wavelengths
of happy and sad
all at different frequencies
for some of us it takes time
to move on from the highs to the lows
and for others,
these changes are
sudden and abrupt
i guess no one is ever fully
satisfied emotionally
because these feeling are never constant
they are like the weather
never completely same the next day
and never, really, completely like the forecast.

i stand on the scale everyday
at first we had a love-hate relationship
and as the numbers started decreasing
i unconsciously let it define my worth
and we got pretty close to being best friends
but like an addict
i relapsed
into a spiral of self-sabotage
doing nothing made me tired
suddenly, i didn't know what i liked
most days i starved my body when guilt seeped through
and on some days i inhaled all the trash
thinking my body craved it
i loathed going out
and staying in suffocated me
it felt like no place was mine
no place was safe
i had cry corners all over the house
and episodes of hyperventilation
that felt like near death
i talked to people
but none knew the whole story
just pieces
and advices that didn't work
i was tired,
exhausted,
guilty
and in intense shock
of reaching a low
i hadn't imagined
nor thought i deserved

but like some addicts
i found my rehab
my safe space
my feeling of little
heaven in a massive hell
i got help
but to reach the finish line
i had to start by myself
one step after the other
it was tiring to run those miles
couldn't feel my legs at some point
but i had cheerleaders on the sidelines
and a little strength to push
right till the finish line
for myself
and no other.

i just need the respect
of being a human
who can have bad days
and outbursts
i am not all sunflowers and lilies
i have a little poison
just like every human
so, give me the space
to be me
without burying me in expectations.

i tried

i am tired

i will try again tomorrow.

sometimes i feel my life is like a snow globe

people see all confetti

and pretty places

but it is still an airtight container

with everything under water

waiting for the next admirer

to shake it hard enough

to disturb the peacefully laid out confetti from the surface.

these days
showering feels like a chore,
even brushing
i'd like to lay in bed
a little longer
just until the light turns to darkness
and then to light again,
i'd like to exist in this nothingness
for a while.

i think for the earth
we've become loose change
trying to get rid of the weight
whenever possible.

my therapist told me that i am doing better

why?
because i am now able to anticipate
the arrival and departure of my sadness

how?
with the help of some anti-depressants
a few self-help books
putting an end to feeling sorry for myself
trying not to assume that my closest friends
are unavailable to help
and found my triggers

in the beginning
i refused to accept
that i was not okay
as the panic attacks
changed their status
from rare to often
i had to ask for help
or entrain that thought

it took a while to find the right therapist
to be precise
it took 5 months,
4 panic attacks,
3-4 breakdowns per week,
feeling of emptiness,
isolating myself from people,
unintentional hunger strikes,

sudden 3-day binging,
fear of falling asleep at night,
anxiety induced tummy aches
a visit to the psychiatrist,
a visit to a psychologist,
2 sessions with my doctor,
a huge breakdown after christmas
in front of my parents
in a house full of 10 guests,
and a sleep-paralysis-lucid-dreaming-nightmare
which made me run to my mom at 2 am

so do me a favour
if you are going through
even 1% of these things
get help
let your friends decide for themselves
how available they want to be for you

the voltage fluctuation in your body
is a sign
the exhaustion without actively doing anything
is a sign
anger, sadness and agitation
is a sign.

as humans
we need connections,
we need other humans
and we need to interact
in order to feel alive

and survive the intensities
of our emotions.

as a reflex action
to feeling anxious,
stressed
or nervous
i, slowly, peel away the skin on the side
of my right thumb nail
with my index finger
layer by layer

this activity is often unconsciously done
because somehow it eases the feeling
and if not, moments later
the wound starts stinging

it is just a consequence
of my anxiety
but it becomes a small inconvenience
for a few days

first i could control it
then it became a habit
and now i am trying to get rid of it
so if you see my thumb in bandaids sometimes
know that i am trying to change
consciously, this time.

i like being alone
but i suffer from loneliness.

i fear losing people
even before knowing them
can you really miss a stranger?

my biggest fears which are also triggers now;
death,
old age,
deadlines,
lizards,
falling in love
and dropping my ice cream on the floor.

insecurities

i couldn't see myself growing
until i believed i was
and just like that
it was quick and complicated
at the same time
see, no one tells you that
you will go through a heartbreak or two
your teeth will probably not be aligned
or you will he hairy in places you don't want to be
no one tells you that from emotionally unavailable
you will become available
relationships will end
and you might have issues after every
but that's growth
isn't it?
no one tells you that society will put you
under a microscope
and you will feel insecure
picking flaws rather than the simple perfections
no one tells you that there will be times
when in a room full of people, you will feel alone
and sometimes when you are alone
you might be the happiest
no one tells you that it will feel like a climb of the everest
to grow
and you will do that throughout life
but one thing they prepare you
for is taking the pressure
and the truth of the world is experiences
when you finally leave home

but don't let your insecurities magnify
don't let your dreams fade
while you learn to be you,
the new you
while you learn all these little things
there will be times you spend overthinking
about the past of who you were
but remember the future you
is kind.

i wonder if you ever think about me
you know, sometimes
in your simple routine
i wonder not because
i miss you
because i want to know
if even
i am worth remembering,
important enough
to be in your memories of the past.

when we are hurt
by someone we love
all we think about is
love is just a ruse
that whatever time
we spent with that someone
has been us living in our delusion
that feels like reality
we dwell on their words
that are often just words with no meaning
birthed from heated arguments
we look for their name to pop up on our screens
emails, socials, texts or just that one facetime for closure
we take time,
space,
but we move on
so why is it we long for the same attachment with someone
new?
if love is just a ruse
then why do we fall into that trap
again and again
and yet hope that someone new
will fill that longing?
we have glued together the pieces we found
but they will
fill the spaces of the small, broken
lost pieces of our heart?
will reciprocate that emotional dependence?
will fix the injuries of the past
and tend to our recovery
with their love

hopefully, unconditionally
and forever?

how do i tell you
i am in love with you
when i know you don't romanticise us?
what words do i use to tell you subtly
and what do i expect out of it?
i am not in love with myself
how will you ever be?
i am not enough for you
how will i ever for another man?
my heart is in pieces
but all the broken parts belong to people
now only my soul is looking for another
who is too out of pieces to give of his heart
and what is left
are two souls
waiting for each other
maybe that is what soulmates
are, when nothing is left
you find a soul
that becomes
everything
and together
you mould
a whole
unbroken heart.

dead flowers and dusty books
that is how i feel from the inside
resting for years with my essence
slowly and silently decaying
you forgot to read me
and water me
and care for me like you promised
the first time we met
initially you took out hours
and then it changed to minutes
now rarely you look at me
and think not of my beauty
but the space i take.

i know you hate your
coffee stained teeth
and your back dimples and your curves
but there is something poetic about it
it is like god wrote a poem
in human form
to tell the world
they may not be a poet
but what they wrote is beautiful
and timeless.

you inspire me
and sometimes i am in awe
of how i got so lucky
to have the privilege of your existence
at the exact time
when i am
and where i am
so, know that
you are enough
you are worth it
and what you think are your flaws
are actually what i love the most.

i am not looking for someone
who will give me butterflies
and sing me to sleep,
just a someone
who will pull me into reality
and push me into euphoria
like a balancing act
someone who will hug me by surprise
and tease me like it is routine
not someone who will apologise in fights
but someone who will hold my hand
to calmly exhale and inhale with me
so we don't say the wrong words
i don't want a romance novel
just someone i deserve
because it has taken me a long time to ask this
for myself,
as i learn about myself.

i am falling in love with you
i don't think i have the courage
to say these words out loud
because i am afraid that
you will not love me back
and i don't think my heart can take it
it is hurting and healing everyday
and hoping that you might say it
before i gather the courage to
but maybe my silence
and your hesitance
will save me from a heartbreak.

is it so hard to love me
to think that i am enough for you?
or is it just you
who has no love to give
because you've been broken before?
i wish i could heal you for us
but what if you don't want us,
maybe just another person that is not me?
what is it that makes anyone hesitant to love me?
is it my body?
is it my mind?
is it the way i look when i cry
or laugh?
is it my teeth
or my nose?
is it my intellect
or my disinterest in some things that they might like?
i can question myself all day
but all is ask is
for some to love me
just the way i can love them
so i don't have to be afraid
to love.

i am the sun
bright on the outside
and burning in my own skin
on the inside
don't come too close
all flesh and bone
will turn to ash
don't go too far
because i can't warm you
just be there
in the comfortable distance
because i don't want to play the odds
of you either completely loving me
or completely hating me
so, for now, i am happy with
our comfortable distance
just to be with you.

your body is a map
from the moment you are born
as you discover
grow and fall
your body changes
the curves and edges
some appreciated
some disliked
but nobody is perfect
so instead of fitting into sizes
fit into a lifestyle you desire
let your body work and change
according to the way you want to live
as long as it remains healthy,
nourishes you and your soul
it took me a long time to realise that
reading about body positivity
from women on media
helps your insecurities a little
but it is your acceptance
towards your body
that kills insecurities
you can tone it as you want
go on diets and exercise as you want
but all bodies are unique and equal
all bodies are perfect
and since you define perfect
be confident
of your rough edges
your different shades in different parts
your river lines

and hotspots
your forest
and your desert
it is your map
be you
i am trying to be me too.

is it me?
can you see that i am faking all that confidence?
or is it my sadness
that with me has consumed you too?
i know i can be crazy
but can't you be that with me?
can we share a few drinks and kisses
and maybe it is enough for the moment?
i've been looking for you in places
and collecting all my love for you
whoever you are
hoping it'll be enough for a lifetime
for the both of us
all i ask is you stay
even when it's hard to deal with me
when i get old and wrinkled
when my bones depend on your arms
to get to places
when i forget to get you flowers
and when the food has no salt
i hope it won't be hard to love me then
if you can love me a little now
overlooking all my setbacks
and insecurities
overlooking the parts that i play for people
and only completely understand me.

there is no need to explain
who and how you love.

i am weak that way, you know
i have all these strong opinions
and awareness of self
and the world
and i still feel helpless
i will easily let the
people i love
walkover me
because i am afraid to lose people
because that is all i've got
people who i can love and share my stories with
people who sometimes miss me
people with who i have arguments with
but they always show up
so, yes, i tend to let the hurt slide
because people are all i've got.

intimate conversations

we sit miles apart
across oceans
only to be met
by the moon
the skies pray
to the heavens
for us to meet
and the stars,
our little love letters,
shooting amidst the dark
patiently waiting
to see us closer
i wish i could drown in your eyes
and sink into your bones
and feel our souls
touching each other
but we have these miles between us
i hope the earth swallows them
because, darling, the universe is rooting for us
and i don't want to disappoint.

i'm in love with you
and i think you know it
but i will never say it to you
because then it becomes real
knowing that i can never have you
but only lose me in you,
knowing i can never be with you
except in my thoughts,
knowing i can never touch you
the way i want to,
knowing that everyday
i will have to let you go
from an imagined future that
will hurt even more
so let it be
a secret or a lie to fool my heart
because what is even love if it is not you.

it is ironic
how we live in a world full of romantics
who claim that romance is dead.

i don't know
if you know that
i think of you
when i am vulnerable
when i am happy
when i am just feeling feelings
i tend to see you in people
and things
and sometimes the sun reminds me
of the conversations
we had till daybreak
and the moon reminds me of our sleepless nights
i have this unhesitant attachment to you
and i am not intentionally in love with you
but maybe in a different world
you'd be too
for now we are neither lovers
nor partners
we are just in the space between the two
laying a middle ground in this world
of extremes.

it's the way you place a kiss
on my forehead
and look into my eyes
it's the way you smile
and catch glimpses of me
it's the way you touch me
like giving love letters a life.

shakespeare is famous
partly because of his writing
but mostly because
he deemed tragedy in love
he did the reverse of
happy endings
and the world applauded it
because in every corner
there was a forgotten love
a lost love
a hard-to-get love
and most of all
a love that never got the chance to love
and maybe that is why
shakespeare is famous.

when you look at me
naked and exposed
i am still hiding
and pretending
because just looking at my naked body
doesn't give you the roadmap
to my mind,
my feelings
and my soul
but when i strip down my heart for you,
my naked heart will let you know that
i desire you,
envy the person who takes up all the space in your heart
and need you to be there
because when you are not
it feels like a moonless night
with even the stars hidden
behind grey clouds.

warm bodies

and shivering hearts

for i fear the miles between us

won't make the pretty sunset skies

feel pretty anymore

rain wouldn't be romantic

and little things would be forgotten easily

if i can't bleed in your eyes

and you can't overflow in my arms

where do we go

when we are tired in our minds

i guess, this is what happens

when there is love

but no way to live it.

i want you to want me
like sun on your skin on a
cold winter day,
i want you to want me
like morning coffee
that makes your hangover
a little less intense,
i want you to want me
like wind in the autumn trees,
i want you to want me
like stars in the sky
for people to admire,
i want you
to be addicted
to my love,
just enough,
not too much,
that you need it
every now and then.

we are like darkness and light
but i promise to meet you at dawn
the oceans and the skies never meet
but whisper to the clouds
our love,
it's like we are two trains
in opposite directions
only catching glimpses of each other
but never collide.

i like how your fingers brush against my skin
i like how they find its way from my pelvis
to my ribs
and then my neck
i feel your hands grabbing my waist
i feel your heart race with my cold hands on your chest
and suddenly our problems seem to disappear
all there is, are two beating hearts,
racing at the same pace
i've waited for these nights to come by sooner
because i've missed you since you left
leaving me
and every inch of my body
craving for your touch,
your glance
and your essence
've missed how my fingers interlocked in yours,
your soft kisses,
your teasing touches
and your caresses
i've missed looking into your eyes
and listen to unsaid words
i've missed guessing your thoughts
while the sentences that left your lips said otherwise.

i want you fingers to slowly move
from my thighs to my ribs
caressing its way through every scar and insecurity
that fades away when i am with you
i want your fingers to linger on my body
just long enough that it makes my thoughts fade
i want you to want me,
my soul and my body
just hold me closer tonight under the stars
and promise me you'll
do it every night
for the moon that's admiring our love
and the earth that's gambling on
our romance,
we chose each other tonight
and i hope we do it every night
because your love consumes me,
it makes me better,
wiser
and makes my heart feel whole
so, darling, hold me closer tonight
and love me like that all the other nights
because i want this,
you and us.

we were lovers
but only secretly
to tell ourselves
that we were living a lie
but i let myself feel
it was real only
for a few seconds
here and there
even though i knew
it wasn't constant or forever
i told myself it was real when
you held my hand
or when we cuddled
sometimes even when we kissed
i let go of myself for just those moments
and as soon as those moments ended
i wrapped my heart in paper,
kept it on your bedside
and fooled my brain into
thinking it was just a dream
that you and i,
us,
are just lies i tell myself
to feel something.

as i am stripping away my layers
one by one
i am also letting you in
i am letting you see all
the imperfections
that feed my insecurities
there is one part of me
hoping that you don't notice them
but at the same time,
please do
at this point i am naked
and willing to be judged
as you lay your eyes on
all the reasons to leave
please, just hold on to that
one which makes you stay
for my heart is fragile
my knees are weak
and my lips are trembling
it's only seconds of waiting
but it feels like hours
when you finally decide
if you want this with me
for the rest of your life
or just one night.

take me to places
not your favourite
i wouldn't want to disturb
the peace you share with it
maybe, we find a new place
where our memories will share the same moments
not less, not more
just the simple minutes
of you and i
in our newfound place.

i share sunsets and carrot cakes
wishes and t-shirts
fries and memories
words and warmth
i'll even give you my love
to gamble with
but please be hesitant.

growing

if only time could stop
and i could breathe in this moment
slowly and deeply
with every sense alive
and keep it in a
little box of memories to
only live it again
when i miss you
because time
steals our memories
and sometimes
our people
and you,
i cannot lose
you to time.

i hope that today your coffee tastes good
and your hair just fall perfectly
i hope when you see yourself in the mirror today
you admire your beauty for a few more seconds
i hope the deadlines that you have to meet get extended so you
stress a little less
i hope you give yourself time to breathe
i hope when the sun sets the clouds look like pink cotton
candy
i hope you enjoy your dessert
and there is someone who checks up on you
i hope the full moon looks so perfect in the starry night
and when you look at it,
you have someone to hold on to
i hope you fall asleep in someone's arms
and wake up to a brighter day
i hope today revisits you tomorrow
and the day after that
until it becomes every day.

like the tides,
i rise
i move forward
and hit the rocks
and then i go back,
back to being a part of the ocean
because it is where i belong
and then i do this again and again
i escape a little
only to crash into rocks
that send me back to the waters.

she was art
abstract at first
as we made it to
our second coffee
i was an admirer of this art
the layers
the lines and curves
the hues
and the beauty when it all came together
it felt intimate
after a few years
she felt like the starry night
or rembrandt's creation
worthy of a museum which i visit everyday
just staring at it for hours
i became an art lover
and she teased me
while i misunderstood it
made my mind run marathons
and my heart feel
i could see
what the artist wanted the world to see
which only a fool would stray eyes from
and i was one of many who would die for.

on rainy days
sometimes
i look forward
to the sunny days
other times
i get drenched.

and when our eyes meet
in a room full of people,
the space between us
is an existence of a parallel universe
because in that universe
it is just you and i
and everything else is
background noise.

i am recollecting the
pieces of me
like people do with memories
hopefully this time
when i put them back together
it won't be hollow.

"once upon a time
in a faraway land"
is the delusion of love
but what is love?
as someone who has only understood it
through art and people
i think love is when
the longing for human touch
intensifies
when the heart thinks
and the mind beats
when their time consumes you
and their words
complicate you
but also simplify you
when you look at a blurry mirror
and all you see is perfection
love is one emotion
you feel constantly
until your bones decay
you either long for it
or have it
but oh, the real love
the love of your life
kind of love
is all these things
and comfort
of being the worst version of yourself
until you decide to be your best
with that person

it is the ease of being you
pure and unchanged
it is the calm you
feel even in a storm
and the anxiety
in a silent room
where the train of your thoughts leave
from station to station,
but you remain at that platform
where amidst a violent crowd,
you feel safe
it is breaking your heart into
pieces and asking them to fix it
and trusting they will.

broken people
mend souls
please thank them
with your whole heart.

you can't hurt me
i overcame depression.

i chose to be chaos
when the world got silent
and i chose questions
to fight the boundaries you set
i chose knowledge
to understand the dichotomy
i chose raised voices
to strangle systems
that became less traditions
and more oppressions
i chose awareness
to corrode minds
with ailing perspectives
i treated disagreement
with normalisation of changes in this century
i chose to be part of the present
and not play by the past.

i watched a bird
don't know what kind,
but i watched it bring little sticks to its nest
i watched it sip water from puddles
and then look around
as if someone was watching her
i watched it call out for other birds
i watched it lay eggs
and stay still for days
or at least when i watched it
and then finally, i saw her little babies
and her first flight for them,
every woman is a bird
free and giving,
homely and nomadic,
deciding where to fly,
and when to make a nest.

i want to be like the wind
take charge and move in directions
that i decide,
i want to be like the sun
always showing up
even on the cloudy days,
i want to be like the stars
making nights feel safe
and holding on to belief,
i want to be like the trees
strong with roots wherever you sow,
i want be like the ocean
wild and humble,
i want to be stoic and in awe
of people
things and places,
i want to feel alive
not just in moments
but the present,
i want to be me
unearthed and bold.
i want to cross over and take leaps
and be a catalyst of my dreams,

i want to be love
and give
till i reach heaven
to be birthed again.

the strings of my heart
are a little old and worn
because they have been used
to perform for many people
in many places
but it has become a bit rusty
just sitting in a corner of my room catching dust
waiting for someone to tune it again
and strum the right strings
until then
i have decided to fix it up
and make it worth the wait.

i hope that this time
the universe colludes with me
and fate works on the script
that i have so generously edited
i hope the negativity
that i have so delicately pushed
to the edge of the black hole
gets sucked into disappearance.

change is how life is supposed to be lived
by finding comfort in the uncomfortable
provoking the uncertainty of the future
and unknowing the past.
the world has yet to witness
your greatness
your talent your kindness
and your compassion
i know it was worth wait
because you carry change
your harness it
and you lead it
for one or many
but you make a difference
so keep collecting droplets of change
one day it will become an ocean.

be patient
my mind is under reconstruction.

when i die
promise to bury me
in grass near the ocean
and with seeds to grow into tress
so that i become useful
before the earth swallows me
my essence remains
in the falling leaves
that submerge in the ocean
when the wind is strong
my tree branches remain the resting place for snow in winters
and in the summers
i am happiness
for the kid that climbs on me
to pick fruit
and shade for ice creams to melt slowly
in little hands
and maybe i can be a home
for birds or squirrels
or letters of the lovers
i hope, when i die
i am useful.

"i am proud of you"
i have wrapped these words
around my neck
sending it all the way
through my spine
to my toes
because i need to feel these words
that i so dedicatedly taught myself
to say out loud
in order to withstand
a world that has forgotten these words exist
forgotten the power they hold
forgotten to say it enough times
for people to heal.

letters

to my sisters,
i know you have this urge to
be better
over perform
and over achieve
but don't let that take away life from you
you have anxieties
that are hard to describe
and patience was never your strong suit
but listen now
that part will be over soon
you'll be okay
i know you expect too much
from yourself,
just lower the bar
it'll help you reach further,
i know you are
rebellious
and strong
and plotting against the society's farce
but do let people in
to feel your tenderness
tell me was society a burden
for you when we were kids?
or has it now caused distress
of getting that job,
meeting the one,
looking flawless
and not expecting too much
i hope your insecurities don't take the better of you
and you learn to self-love

and put yourself first
even in hard situations
i hope you realise that beauty
is unique, it is different
and it is you
i hope you know
that you give me strength
and stability
even on the stormy days
i know, like me,
you have struggles too
and the daily battles you stand through
has built walls around you
but let the close ones
see glimpses of your vulnerability
and support you
because you are not alone
like always,
i have your back
i hope you give yourself time and space
to grow and reflect
and are not always under the pressure
to be better
i know it gets hard sometimes
so let yourself go and cry
vent
or even ask for help
i know you crave to be loved
to feel it
and see it
and not only listen to just words that don't touch you

i am proud of you
for the woman you have become
and eagerly waiting to see
how you create a life
for the woman you want to be
i ask of you only this
when you start questioning yourself
look at the people around you
the lives you have changed or touched
and know that your existence is a privilege for us
i hope you feel alive and enjoy the tiny moments of life
and the big moments of freedom
i hope you know that i love you
and a piece of my heart stays with you
at all times and every day.

to my bestfriend,
tell me how you are so content
how you stress
but it tends to leave
too quickly
how you are sometimes
all over the place yet still
composed
how your principles
never waver
even for a second
is it hard?
to be a man in this world
that keeps pushing responsibilities
on your young shoulders
tell me how even in
chaos you find calm
is it not consuming
to always feel needed
and only rarely ask
people of their time?
is it exhausting
to shape shift
into unwanted roles
and exchange pretences every now and then
because it is your duty
that society has very eloquently
burdened you with?
have you witnessed
acts of love

and being loved
and have they fulfilled you?
how does it feel to have successes
to hold onto?
and the failures just walk by
with you undisturbed
or at least that's what it looks like from afar
i hope you feel alive
in moments and on days
and the world never gets to you
like it has to many
i hope you know
you are adored
and loved
and even a slightest bit
admired
how is it
you are never quick to judge
but only learn
how is it to have opinions
and anger
and misdirection
but always be at the right path
teach me how you let go
of distress
and manage to find comfort in change
i hope you know
you are adored
and loved
and even a slightest bit
admired.

to my grandparents,
i know there have been drastic changes for you
and it is hard to accept change when you are forced to learn
new ways
of the new working world
but i admire you
for learning and growing even as you grow old
i admire you dadu
to adjust with change,
just like that lights turned off
before abandoning rooms of your habits
i admire you dadi
for accepting my rebellious way of living
for making sure to be a part of a society
for keeping yourself sane
i know, like every mother
you are unsatisfied with how things are
i see, that slowly,
you are losing patience
i am sorry
for not realising that while
i was growing up i made it seem like
i was growing out of love for you
but i promise,
i think about you at times when
i miss home or reminisce
my childhood
i see how age is catching up on you and
i hate it
because while we all grow

at different paces and different stages
i hope that age doesn't pace for you
i hope it wanders and loses its way
thank you
for loving me even in my worst phases
and not forcing your beliefs
and society's expectations
and supporting me while
i explore
i don't think i have said it enough
but maybe i start saying it now
i love you.

to my dad,
i have this faint memory
of you holding me tightly
in your arms while running down the stairs
i now understand
that there was an earthquake that day
but somehow you are always
there holding me again
tightly in your arms
when i feel like the earth is
shaking under me
and that's one of my favourite memories
i also remember
listening to music on *mtv*
every evening
in a room that might seem small now
but at that time it had everything i needed
in the whole world
that's my other favourite memory
i also remember the email
where you said you were proud of me
when i did well in school
i want to always remain that person for you
but i think all my memories with you
are my favourite like
when you taught me to bike and i fell,
like that day we played football
for just a few minutes in the rain,
like when you wrestle with me

and hug me at times
i am grateful that you never
made me feel that
i was any less than a boy
and now you make me feel
i am worth much more than a man
you have taught me the importance
of patience,
humour
and hard work
although i am not really good at the last part
but i am working on it
thank you for making me feel like an adult
and letting me figure out adulting
in my own way
you have always been my inspiration
not because how you made a life for us
but because you taught us to be happy in
what we have
and earning the things we want
thank you,
papa.

to my mum,
if it weren't for you
i wouldn't have found what i am good at
i wouldn't have found
swimming
writing
travelling
as passions to follow
nor would i have the courage
because you too taught me that too
i know, like you
perfectionism isn't a trait i have
but from you i know how to survive
ironically,
we have both struggled emotionally
a lot
and that is our point
where we meet into agreement
because on the rest of the
things we often disagree
i am grateful to you for
teaching me survival
be it emotional, physical or mental
i am grateful to you
for you gave me
the most tangible and
irreplaceable gift, my sister
i am grateful to you
for raising me as your daughter

because even though
i don't believe in god
i do believe the universe wanted me
to have you
i am also sorry
because sometimes
i don't hug you back or hang up
and fight like a teenager
but you are one person
i will always return to and
that's all the reasons
you have given me to love you
even though i don't need reasons
but thank you,
mumma.